BRUNKOW CHEESE OF WISCONSIN!

●●○ Floriole Bakery & Cafe

Radical Root Organic Farm

Bennisons Bakery

KINNIKINNICK FARM

SEASONS SODA

Compost Center

Shana Wilson

AMAZING SHRIMP
HAREK WOLANOWSKI

Nichols Farm

Hillside Orchards
and
Hillside Chestnut Orchards
Rebecca Brandt
Paul Thelen Owner
daughter

Majestic Nursery & Farm

Hoosier Mama
PIE COMPANY

Abby's
Crepes

GREEN ACRES FARM
Since 1933
agata

PASTA
PUTTANA!

Al Bekkum
Nordic Creamery

Joel

Beth Myron
+ ava

Heartland
Meats

Genesis
Growers

Kings
Hill Farm

Matt Hoffman
Matt's Urban Garden

CRUMB
* ANNE
BR

In Memory of

Abby Mandel

Without her there would be no Green City Market

Dedicated to

Kim Bartko
Sarah Stegner
and Holly Sherr

Without each of them there would be no book

Green City Market
A Song of Thanks

Green City Market Reflections: *Rick Bayless* Frontera Grill
Sarah Stegner Prairie Grass Cafe
Paul Virant Vie, Virant
Carrie Nahabedian Naha, Brindille
Bruce Sherman North Pond
Kim Bartko Food Activist
Beth Eccles Green Acres Farm
Tracey Vowell Three Sisters Farm
Paul Kahan Blackbird, The Publican
Jeanne Nolan Edible Gardens
Bill Kim urbanbelly, bellyQ
Donna La Pietra and *Bill Kurtis*
Abby Schilling Mick Klug Farm
Melissa Flynn Green City Market
Holly Sherr Abby Mandel

3

Rick Bayless
Frontera Grill,
Xoco, Leña Brava,
Topolobampo

Probably most of you know—though some may find it a surprise—that modern Chicagoans haven't always had access to locally grown produce.

No, two decades ago, it wasn't common to have access to the tiny, tender strawberries from a local farm at the end of May, or those strikingly aromatic peaches in July, or dozens of varieties of apples—from rusty-looking ancient heirlooms to modern cultivars with perfect sweet-tart balance—throughout the fall. Twenty-some years ago, most of us had read about diminutive mesclun salad greens popularized by Alice Waters in Berkeley, California, but we wouldn't have known where to purchase some to pass around at our own dining tables. In fact, when I settled in Chicago in the mid-80s, there were no farmers markets at all. Grocery stores and, for chefs, the South Water produce terminal, provided us with everything we ate. And pretty much every fruit and vegetable and herb we knew about was in season every day of the year. And none of it was harvested anywhere near where we lived.

By the 90s, the San Francisco Bay area chefs had settled into cooking with remarkably tasty, enticingly unusual ingredients that were being cultivated for them by small farms that thrived in the area's moderate climate. "Could we ever be able to jump on that bandwagon?" some of us wondered. Could the Chicagoland area ever boast farms that would inspire local chefs and home cooks the way they did in the Bay area?

When New York City started sprouting farmers markets full of produce from the Hudson Valley, a much more challenging climate than California, a core of us were sure we could will into existence a movement of small local farms supplying markets and restaurants around Chicago.

Led by Abby Mandel, a nationally recognized food writer and culinary educator, we started taking steps to turn dreams into reality.

A couple of fledgling farmers markets had taken up weekly residence in Chicago and a good number of people were filtering through and filling bags with produce that was fresher and more varied than they had ever seen. But we knew that for this happy trend to become an essential way of life, we needed more. We needed a market packed with farmers who grew enough unique produce to attract chefs (chefs have buying power and relish in introducing their guests to new tastes). We needed a market that would reflect our group's commitment to sustainable agriculture as a viable model for the future. And we needed a market that could serve to share knowledge, inspiring everyone who likes to eat to enjoy the bounty of what our local farmers have harvested from their healthy tended soil.

You wouldn't have known any of that from Green City Market's first season. It was six farmers in an alley on the south side of the Chicago Theater. Hardly anyone came. Still, clear and hopeful vision is a hard thing to squelch. We eventually settled into the southern end of Lincoln Park and started building Green City Market in earnest. As each growing season trailed inevitably, sadly, toward dormancy, everything was reborn full of hope before we knew it the following spring. Just like our market. Each year we had more farmers who had figured out how to have more early-season vegetables as well as ones that could be offered later and later in the fall. Each year we had more chefs and home cooks who had discovered the fulfillment of participating in our burgeoning local agriculture, preparing our season's fruits and vegetables, grown by folks they knew.

The next thing we knew, connecting to local agriculture became a thing. "Farm to table" was on everyone's lips, even if they didn't understand much about local farms or how to transform local produce for their tables. Still, everyone came on Wednesdays and Saturdays to wander the farmers' booths, snack on crepes with local veggie fillings and buy vibrant flavors to filter into dishes, flavors that reminded them that Chicago could boast of more than legendary architecture and sports teams.

For a number of years, any young chef opening a restaurant in Chicago was taken only as seriously as the list of farm names on his or her menu. "Farm to table" became so commonplace that it was no longer definitive. Which, for some, meant that we'd accomplished our goal, right? The problem was that everything had happened really fast.

Many of the farms hadn't yet grown to a truly viable size. The importance of buying locally hadn't yet become an integral part of every culinary school program, of every chef's kitchen. And many of us still hadn't settled into an irresistible anticipation of those local strawberries, peaches and apples, those local herbs, tomatoes and myriad fall squash. Fully realizing our goal of a vital local agricultural economy, of abundant and accessible ingredients, of a Chicagoland that unanimously celebrates the uniqueness of our region's specialties, remains very much a work in progress.

As Green City Market heads into its third decade, we are thrilled with how far we've come. Yet we recognize that it's taken us only onto the first rung on a ladder that rises toward the full expression of "local and sustainable." We stand at the ready to share our passion, our commitment with an ever widening audience of chefs and home cooks. All with an unwavering confidence that each step we take makes our communities better places to live.

Inspired by the authentic experience of the Mexican kitchen, Chef Rick Bayless has achieved international acclaim and thrilled North American audiences at every level—from the elegant artistry of Topolobampo and Frontera Grill, both recipients of the James Beard Foundation's award for Outstanding Restaurant, to the street-food fiesta of Xoco and Leña Brava, Baja-inspired and wood-fired. Chef Bayless is renowned as a gifted teacher, and his distinctive vision and boundless enthusiasm instill the Frontera team with a passion for great food and exceptional restaurant experience.

A recipient of the Julia Child Foundation award and multiple James Beard Foundation awards for culinary leadership, he continues to be an active member of the board of directors for Chicago's Green City Market.

*T*wenty years ago, I helped start Chicago's Green City Market with Abby Mandel at the lead. I was working at the Ritz Carlton Chicago, had just received my first James Beard Award, and was—and still am—totally committed to bringing the best, most delicious food to the table of my restaurant. It only made sense to source the food that is freshest, at the peak of season, and carefully grown. Access was a barrier for Chicago chefs, and for its citizens; Abby's answer to solving this problem was to start Green City Market. Her passion and commitment to make this market thrive was intense. She put all her years of knowledge, contacts, and leadership into making it something sustainable for the Midwest. She worked to set an example for both the outlying Chicago area, and the whole nation, of how great a market could be. As Green City Market grew, it helped establish a very supportive and highly functioning food community, one that is still going strong, twenty years later!

Here are some of the principles that distinguish Green City Market, give it an identity, and make it unique…besides the incredibly beautiful setting in Chicago's Lincoln Park, of course.

Preserving the face of the farmer: The direct contact that the market offers the people of Chicago establishes a valuable personal relationship with the farmer, creating a sense of community. The farmers work so hard and need to have viable incomes to continue their work. They need to be afforded the respect they all deserve for working the precious land that surrounds us and provides the bounty that sustains us. It is also amazing to have them in front of their produce, to answer the buyer's questions: What is coming into season? Which crops are bountiful and at peak flavor? What is near its end? How should I store this? How do I prepare this to nourish myself and my family?

The farmers not only protect our land, our access to good healthy food, and our heirloom seeds that have been passed down from generation to generation, but face-to-face, they can share their knowledge—much of which has been forgotten by the rest of us.

Third-party certification: All the farmers at Green City Market are committed to protecting the earth. Let that settle in. What does it really mean? There is no way for someone who hasn't worked the earth to truly understand the effort, hardship, and calculated risks that the farmers experience while bringing us the food on our tables. Third-party certification is a formal system that validates their efforts; it protects them from people questioning the integrity of what they do. Many people don't even realize that these certifications go above and beyond "organic." Third-party certifiers look at fair wage, protection of top soil, integrated wild life, protection of the watershed, and more.

Edible Garden and food education: Green City Market has a commitment to teaching people how to grow their food and prepare it. An interactive, edible teaching garden, run by Jeanne Pinsof Nolan, sits inside the Lincoln Park Farm Zoo. All schools in Chicago have an invitation to take a tour of the garden, giving the children an opportunity to plant or harvest depending on the time of year. It's a beautiful "work of art" that is functional and highly effective at getting the word out about how to grow your own food. We also have recently started teaching directly in schools. We need young passionate students who have the potential to be leaders in our communities and who also value and appreciate the source of their food. Teaching in the schools has so many positive effects on the students and their families, and ultimately impacts the future of the market itself.

Here's the reason Green City Market and buying local is important: Farmers in our area need to have access to a thriving market, in order to provide them with income that supports a healthy life style, and for their critical job to be a viable career option. We can ensure that future generations have access to healthy and abundant food grown in proximity to where we live. Our local farmers protect the land and diversity of edible plants with their knowledge of how to grow and harvest them. They are the critical link between us and the nourishment that sustains us. We are fortunate that the Midwest has such abundance. The seasons offer variety and renewal each year. I am inordinately grateful for the hard work each farmer puts into the land. Green City Market provides the link between the farmer, the chef, and the people of Chicago.

A personal note on Abby Mandel: Our founder was also my friend. When something exciting happens at the Green City Market, like the first-of-the-season wild black and red raspberries hit the stands and I can almost taste the slice of pie I'm going to make with them, I still think of her. Wednesdays were great days to stop by her house and hang out in her kitchen. After making the trip down to Green City Market at 7:00 am to get the best of the crop before anyone else, she was cooking up a storm. She might put you to work chopping onions, cleaning beets, boning out a leg of lamb, but she would always feed you. I am proud be a part of the work she started twenty years ago at Green City Market.

Sarah Stegner is Co-Chair of the Board of Directors of Green City Market and one of the original founding members with Abby Mandel. Co-owner of Prairie Grass Cafe in Northbrook, Illinois, she has won two James Beard Foundation Awards, for Rising Star Chef and Best Chef Midwest.

I love the Green City Market because local food rocks! I started shopping at the GCM in 1999, just a year after it opened, when I was working at Everest. Now I'm honored to serve on the GCM board and help support this important farmers market. The Vie and Vistro teams love our hardworking farmer friends and all their awesome goodness!

I fondly recall meeting Abby for the first time; she had a nurturing enthusiasm about her. There was something about her that made you think, "This is the right thing to do"—developing those essential relationships with the farmers, inspiring your culinary creativity, and ultimately having a deeper connection to the land.

GCM not only helped the culinary scene in Chicago, but it built an amazing restaurant community that rivals other cities. For many years, I would pick up Chef Patrick Sheerin every Wednesday on my way to the market and we would shop for both of our restaurants. The camaraderie and relationships, which have been forged through the market, are tremendous. The number of people who are searching for locally produced food has grown exponentially, and the Green City Market has really helped fuel that change—thanks to Abby, the farmers, the chefs and the people who love them!

Since the 2004 opening of Vie and 2014 opening of Vistro, Chef Paul Virant has risen to nationwide acclaim for his contemporary midwestern cuisine emphasizing canned and preserved ingredients. His philosophy of local, seasonal eating stems from techniques he learned on his family's farm in Missouri. In 2017, collaborating with midwestern farmers, Virant launched Jar Sessions, a locally made, small-batch collection of pickled and preserved farm-to-fork produce.

Paul Virant
Vie, Vistro, Jar Sessions

Carrie Nahabedian
Naha, Brindille

Abby Mandel was a culinary force in our city for many years as a cookbook author, syndicated newspaper columnist, food writer and most memorably, the voice and founder of the Green City Market, Chicago's only local and sustainable agriculture market. Abby was tireless in her efforts to make Chicagoans aware of the vast benefits of supporting midwestern farmers and for keeping Chicago "GREEN." Her work has continued to ensure that every household in the city has the availability of serving natural organic products that are grown and harvested using sustainable agriculture.

In 1989, Abby created the Best of the Midwest market that celebrated the best small producers in Illinois and nearby midwestern states. With the assistance of the American Institute of Food and Wine, this one-day event showcased not only produce, but also cheese, meats, fish, wild game, beer and wine. That success inspired her creation, the Green City Market.

The Green City Market is the heart and soul of Abby. She worked "hands-on" to insure its success. In return, the city is blessed with this most exquisite market and social gathering place for chefs, restaurateurs, food lovers and Chicagoland residents. As many can attest, Abby passionately bridged the farmer with the chef. No one could refuse Abby! When she saw that so many Chicago chefs were frequenting the market, she personally asked each chef to do a demonstration class so that the public could witness first-hand how to cook using seasonal products. Every market day, Abby was behind the crepe stand, making several delicious varieties of crepes using the finest, freshest market ingredients. To this day, you can savor Abby's Crepes and all the profits go directly to the market.

Abby headed the committee that inspects each farm to insure the credibility of their sustainable farming techniques and works directly with the farmers to make sure they have what they need to do business in the city. As much as chefs like myself like to come to the market and pick up a few things, we are very fortunate that through the efforts of Abby, the farmers deliver to us several times a week! It was this drive and determination that has made the Green City Market so spectacular and it shows in the growth that the market has achieved each year.

With the initial assistance of Mayor Richard M. Daley, the market is held each Wednesday and Saturday from the spring to late fall in Lincoln Park. Because the demand for product is so high, Abby started the "Winter Market" in the Kovler Lion House in the Lincoln Park Zoo under the watchful eyes of the big cats! Now located in another unique setting, the Peggy Notebaert Nature Museum, this late season market provides an excellent opportunity for customers to procure great products for their holiday tables.

A past Chicago and International President of Les Dames d'Escoffier, Abby was instrumental in raising funds for the market with the assistance of the Chicago chapter. The annual and very popular Chef BBQ is a main source of income for the market. Abby created "Friends of the Green City Market" where individuals are encouraged to support the farmers and market through a small donation. In return, they receive weekly advance updates of market items, seminars by individuals in the "Green" movement and numerous other benefits. Abby is widely remembered and respected here in Chicago as well as nationally. Her *Chicago Tribune* weekly newspaper column was carried from Los Angeles to Dallas and into numerous small markets across America.

Abby was a frequent contributor to *Bon Appétit* magazine where she taught Americans, step by step, the basics of food processor cooking focused on using fresh ingredients to make the simplest meals in a timely manner. She dreamed of making Chicago's Green City Market the best in the country, respected and enjoyed by all.

Chicago magazine honored Abby in 2007 for her vision and for making the Green City Market what it is today. In celebration of the tenth anniversary, Mayor Richard Daley recognized Abby and the market with a City of Chicago proclamation declaring a "Green City Market Day."

Abby's vision has been achieved and then some. She would be so proud to have seen the progress of the past decade in the growth of "farm to table" at our restaurants, but more importantly, the improvement in availability of local, sustainable products now marketed to the public in grocery stores across Chicagoland.

This really has come full circle. The farmers now have more visibility than ever before, which insures their continuation of their profession and passion. Just walk the market and see the enthusiastic faces of the shoppers: Grazing, conversing, shopping, tasting and enjoying the bounty of our Midwest.

After departing her position as Executive Chef of the Four Seasons Hotel Los Angeles at Beverly Hills, Carrie Nahabedian returned to her native Chicago to open NAHA in 2000, which garnered her a James Beard Award and nine consecutive Michelin stars. Carrie opened Brindille in the spring of 2013 along with partner and cousin Michael. Brindille's refined Parisian fare celebrates the Nahabedian cousins' favorite spots in Paris. She is a Chicago girl who loves her City!

*I*t's been such a thrill, treat and reward to have been so intimately involved from the earliest days of the market and to have seen the growth of both the market itself, as well as the awareness of the chefs and public that shop there. Abby was truly a visionary for having understood the void, need, and opportunity to build what has clearly become not only a jewel for the city, but a model market for the country.

Since the inception of the Green City Market twenty years ago, chefs here in Chicago—and the public at large—have come to a much better understanding of the necessary value to place in the provenance of their food. The importance of how something was grown or raised was, and remains, at the heart of the GCM mission, driving much of the oversight of today's market.

It's cool to have been there from the ground up, and to see how current farmers, chefs, and even market staff—many of whom never knew the farmers, chefs and market originals from "back in the day"— value and talk about concerns and products relative to past, present or future growing seasons.

Bravo Abby!

Bruce Sherman is chef and partner at North Pond and has been dazzling diners with his broadly influenced, subtle and seasonal cuisine since 1999. Sherman was honored by *Food & Wine* as one of America's "Best New Chefs" in 2003. He then was nominated six successive years by the esteemed James Beard Foundation in the "Best Chef: Great Lakes Region" category, before ultimately winning the award in 2012. North Pond has also been awarded a Michelin star for the 2014-2019 Red Guide books.

Bruce Sherman
North Pond

On a workday lunch hour dash through the alley behind the Chicago Cultural Center, I stumbled into the very first Green City Market. A handful of tables were clustered in the blazing late-Spring sun. The selection was small but unusual enough to stop me in my tracks. "Could that be mesclun," I wondered? A farmer explained to me what their small group was doing in this odd location and I thought, "How interesting. I hope they're here next week!" None of us in the alley on that May day in 1998 could have anticipated the transformative effect this market would have on Chicago.

What was on your dinner table in 1998? Most of us shopped at grocery chains and never thought twice about where the food came from or how it was grown. Fruit or vegetables fresh from the farm could only be had at a rural farm stand. Whole Foods Market, now seemingly everywhere, had just opened its first Chicago location. The shelves full of organic and natural products in that first small store were a wonderland compared to the handful of dusty bulk bins and wheezing coolers tucked in back of the city's few health food stores which, until then, were Chicago's only source for organic food.

Fast-forward twenty years and Chicago has a vibrant food community—much of it focused on locally grown, sustainably produced food. Relocated to Lincoln Park, Green City Market played a significant role in shaping a community of chefs, food lovers, and the growers and artisan producers who serve them. In turn, this community has gone on to pioneer a model for local economic development that now drives a thriving regional food system of large and small food businesses.

From the first bell pepper seed my kindergarten self sprouted in a paper cup, food has been a transformative force in my own history.

Although I grew up in the suburbs, the deepest taste memories that shaped my passion for cooking and gardening local, sustainable food are connected with the home gardens my grandparents relied on to feed themselves. Autumn visits to apple orchards near our Pennsylvania home meant tart-sweet cider, and the apple pies my mother baked.

Later, these experiences influenced my interests and choices: My book publishing career focused on lavishly illustrated cookbooks and gardening manuals, allowing me to combine my skills in art and design with my passion for cooking and growing food. That's how Sharon Hoogstraten and I forged our professional collaboration and friendship. Together we created many beautiful book projects and it seemed natural we would be interested in a project that involved food.

In June of 2008, we took a Wednesday morning walk through Green City Market—its tables stacked with colorful produce, musicians playing, kids running through the grass, and the sun reflecting off our splendid lakefront—a respite that anyone could enjoy for free. Could we tell the stories of these farmers? Or Abby Mandel's story? Possibly the story of the larger food movement? Our only certainty was that this market had a positive energy for both of us. We hope the results of this visual journey will resonate with and nourish you.

Kim Bartko is an artist, book designer, food activist, and food business consultant. She has served on the board of Growing Home, a nonprofit organization supporting an urban farm and jobs-training program. Working with the nonprofit FamilyFarmed she produced the annual Good Food Festival and also launched and developed the curriculum for its Good Food Business Accelerator. Kim is now a consultant with food tech startups.

I loved Abby Mandel, and the friends that we have made at Green City market have become like family. Our small family farm has survived and flourished thanks to Abby's vision.

I remember the 10th anniversary of the Green City Market so vividly, staring out into the incredible group of people that amassed to celebrate GCM and Abby, and feeling so nervous and emotional. Before we went on the stage alongside Mayor Daley, Rick Bayless, Bill Kurtis, Sarah Stegner and the others, I remember Abby coming over to our booth at the market and her warm embrace, thanking us in advance for being a part of the special ceremony. "Remember to talk about how you arrived here," she reminded us. "People want to know about you, the farmer, and your relationship to the market."

Family history…that part was easy. But then we had the rather overwhelming task of informing this group, in a few short minutes, just how amazing Abby really was in creating a market and an environment that accomplished exactly what she intended it to be—and that would inevitably change our lives and small farm business in ways we never would have imagined.

Trembling and speaking through some tears, we went back to 2001, the year that we joined the market. We told everyone about those early years in Lincoln Park when a few hundred people attended, and the only chefs that visited were Abby's personal friends. Always positive and seeing the possibilities (and putting her arm through mine) she would ask for feedback. How do we reach more people, more chefs, make new connections? I think she knew the answers, but wanted to affirm our commitment, in spite of the "gloomy" markets, and our belief in the future.

Through Abby's encouragement, farmer names were being added to menus. There were dinners, market potlucks, fundraisers that featured GCM farmers alongside local chefs (most memorable for us was being paired with Shaun McClain of Green Zebra at Donna La Pietra and Bill Kurtis' Mettawa estate), chef demonstrations featuring market produce, and eventually the grand GCM BBQ. Having chefs like Paul Kahan, Bill Kim, Carrie Nahabedian, Bruce Sherman, and Sarah walk through our tents felt magical and seeing more and more chefs gather and start their Wednesdays at Green City Market proved that Abby's diligent efforts were paying off. And as more well-known Chicago chefs shopped the market, more people did. Her achievement was to connect local farmers to Chicago chefs and consumers. We are so thankful that she lived to see the transformation from our small beginning.

I will always remember her delight, despite the gravity of her illness, at the success of the 2008 GCM Chef BBQ. I treasure a personal note that we received from Abby dated 30 July 2008: "Dear Beth & Brent, Thank you so much for putting the 2008 Green City Market over the top! You've been the best—no one could do better! Love, Abby." I suspect every vendor got a note. Abby had a special way of making each person she met feel like they made the difference. The significance of the gift she gave us when she asked us to be a part of GCM cannot be overstated.

Along with her husband, Brent, Beth Eccles is co-owner of Green Acres, a third-generation family farm in North Judson, Indiana. They sell their Certified Naturally Grown produce to farmers markets, scores of Chicago restaurants, and May through October at the Green City Market in Lincoln Park.

Tracey Vowell
Three Sisters Garden

*O*ne way or another, I have been involved with Green City Market since its start twenty years ago. In the early days, hosting and attending planning meetings as a chef, joining the application committee and eventually investing, with local producers, in growing the idea of a local food economy that could develop into a thriving marketplace with Green City as the nexus. All the while, I was living on a vegetable farm in Plainfield and getting my feet wet learning the fundamentals of small farming. I eventually transitioned from my chef career into farming, which meant that as I moved from the purchasing side in the local food movement to the producer side, I was still deeply involved in the market, but with a whole new perspective. Back on the application committee, and then briefly on the board of directors as well, I contributed where I could as a farmer participating in the market, and so to help move the market forward as a beacon for locally produced, clean, diverse food.

Not only a wonderful market that steadfastly adheres to the original philosophy of selling only locally produced, sustainably raised agricultural products, Green City is that thriving marketplace where consumers, chefs, grocers and farmers all come together. It is a jewel of dedicated community partners, not only to local food, but to our local economy and midwestern environmental health overall. Green City has been instrumental in the return of good, healthy, locally produced food, offering the bounty of midwestern-produced ingredients, educating home cooks about what to do with those ingredients. This market strives to present options for the consumer regarding sound ecological practices, enlisting market customers to become more knowledgeable and active in preserving our part of the world, the best that we know how, for future generations.

As a chef, I was thankful for GCM because it brought together many local farmers and allowed me to make and present better food for my customers. As a farmer, I am thankful for GCM because it allows me a picturesque venue in which to offer my products, a consistent customer base, a sense of community including meaningful interaction with other farmers and chefs, but also with appreciative shoppers that satisfies a more ethereal social need.

We are lucky to have the Green City Market in Chicago, no matter which side of the farmer/consumer equation we stand on. Our lives are made better by the mere reminder that our food system is made up of a great number of amazing individuals working in unison to present a collective of nutritious, artisanal and familiar foods, enriching our lives by their presence.

After 25 years in kitchens, Tracey Vowell knew it was time for a change, but continuing to be a part of promoting a healthy local food culture was critical. Developing a plan for purchasing directly from farmers as a chef in an extremely busy restaurant, learning about seasonality while working with producers of all sorts, she formed a vision of becoming a small scale vegetable farmer. She slowly began ramping up for the next chapter on a 10 acre plot south of Chicago in Kankakee. Twenty years later, Three Sisters Garden, as a Certified Naturally Grown farm, produces specialty crops, vegetables, and grains, primarily for restaurants in the Chicago area. Working the land is hard, as was the case of the chef career, but the change has certainly been rewarding, allowing for days in the sunshine and the full experience of nature, seasons, and all the satisfaction that comes with it.

I've always garnered great joy from the garden and the woods, so finding myself scouring farmers markets for inspiration and knowledge seemed like the natural way to turn a failed computer science career into a life spent in professional kitchens.

As a young cook, my years with Erwin Drechsler (Metropolis) and Rick Bayless (Frontera Grill, Topolobampo, etc.) revolved around the virtues of Alice Waters and Chez Panisse, as well as formulating a cooking philosophy dependent on seasonality and freshness.

When my partners and I opened Blackbird in 1997, I was shopping the city markets religiously, from Lincoln Square to Federal Plaza. Through those experiences, I developed relationships with several farmers who planned to participate in Abby Mandel's organic market next to the Chicago Theater.

My reaction? Hallelujah! Finally, an organic market!

I also remember a meeting in the basement of Frontera Grill (at Abby's request) with Chefs Rick Bayless and Sarah Stegner. Abby's ambition was to get the Chicago chef community behind the young market. Her visionary concept happened before chefs were the celebrities they are today. The word got out and within a short amount of time, what started as a weekly meeting with a few volunteers evolved into a room filled to capacity with helpful people dedicated to creating the vital community organization the Green City Market is today.

The market has established a lasting connection between chefs and farmers. Those relationships have created countless opportunities for farmers all around the Midwest. I personally believe the Green City Market has created foundational

guidelines for farmers to grow genuinely sustainable produce. Ultimately, the market and farmers working together has created a healthier city for all of us to live in and enjoy.

In 2007, I spent an hour strolling around the market with Alice Waters. I could feel her excitement as she commented that our market had the most diverse product she'd ever seen. It reminded me of something Abby said at the very beginning: If chefs support this market, people will come. Needless to say, that vision has been fully realized, and Chicago's food community and our great city are both better for it.

Over the past twenty plus years, Chef Paul Kahan has become the nationally recognizable face of Chicago chefs. Passionately seasonal, unconventionally creative and dedicated to the inspiration of classical cuisine, Kahan and One Off Hospitality Group have received international acclaim for Blackbird, avec, The Publican, Big Star, Publican Quality Meats, Nico Osteria, Dove's Luncheonette, Publican Quality Bread, Publican Tavern O'Hare, Anker and Pacific Standard Time. Awarded Outstanding Chef by the James Beard Foundation in 2013 and Best Chef of the Midwest in 2004, Kahan has earned the respect of many who claim him to be one of America's most influential working chefs. In 2018, his cookbook *Cheers to the Publican, Repast and Present: Recipes and Ramblings from an American Beer Hall,* won the IACP award in the "Chefs and Restaurants" category. A Chicagoan through and through, Kahan is known for developing relationships with midwestern farmers—leaving a permanent mark on his culinary outlook. Despite the numerous accolades, Kahan regards his work as a mentor for young chefs as one of his greatest accomplishments.

Jeanne Nolan
Edible Gardens

The Edible Gardens is in Lincoln Park Zoo's Farm-in-the-Zoo. It was planted in 2005, and has been maintained by Green City Market since.

In 2004, I had just returned to the Chicago area after spending seventeen years living and working on an organic communal farm. Looking to get involved with the environmental movement that had grown in my absence, I took an assistant job with local foods pioneer and Green City Market founder Abby Mandel.

I'd been working in the Market office (located in Abby's suburban home at the time) for a few months when Abby asked me to drive downtown with her to Lincoln Park Zoo to check out the scraggly thousand-square-foot plot of land in the Farm-in-the-Zoo, located across the street from the market, that we ultimately transformed into The Edible Gardens. Years earlier it had been part of an exhibit, but it had become a forgotten garden with stumps of dead and dying plants. The zoo had offered the site as a possible location for a demonstration garden connected to Green City Market. A stone's throw from the plot was a garden 4 times its size that was already in use, dedicated exclusively, per an agreement with one of the zoo's sponsors, John Deere, to industrially farmed crops such as corn, wheat, alfalfa, and soybeans.

Abby leaned on the picket fence surrounding the smaller plot, smiled with a sly light in her eyes, and said, "Can you do here what you did when you were farming?" She'd been thinking about a project of Alice Waters', The Edible Schoolyard, which had been designed to teach children how food grows and then travels from farm to fork. Abby envisioned something of a live theatre—a garden happening in real time, a place where families could take part in whatever care the growing plants needed, from turning the compost, to pulling up weeds to participating in the harvest: A place for children and families to learn about where their food comes from and how to grow it themselves.

I loved her concept and jumped at the chance to create an interactive, public garden dedicated to Edible Education. The program is still going strong. The Edible Gardens, a 5,000 square-foot urban agriculture project grows in the heart of Lincoln Park Zoo's Farm-in-the-Zoo. As Green City Market's primary educational outreach program, The Edible Gardens' mission is to connect children with their food hands-on, and to ensure that families have the knowledge, experience, and inspiration to help support a sustainable food system. Welcoming over 25,000 visitors annually, the Gardens are open to the public from April through November. Garden educators from The Organic Gardener Ltd. and Lincoln Park Zoo volunteers work together to host school groups, field trips, and adult workshops throughout the season.

Abby's inimitable spirit lives on today in so many ways. Not many days pass without me feeling gratitude for the profoundly positive impact her life has had on Chicago's local food system, the national good food movement, and on my life personally. She was that rare combination of drive, charisma, and a clear mission—a person who creates an everlasting imprint on our World.

Jeanne Nolan has been Director of The Edible Gardens since 2005. She is founder and president of the Organic Gardener Ltd., and author of *From the Ground Up: A Food Grower's Education in Life, Love and the Movement That's Changing the Nation.*

Green City Market is more than a market. It goes so much deeper than that. It's relationships with people who become part of your life. These farmers are family to me.

Before Green City even existed, when I was working at Charlie Trotter's restaurant, I used to go to the farmers market in the parking lot of Lincoln Park High School on Saturday mornings to buy produce. This was around 1993. It's where I first met and got to know Beth Eccles from Green Acres Farm. There was a mutual respect there, and with her being half-Japanese, we could relate well to each other. Beth is like a sister to me now. I've seen her kids grow up. I even hired her daughter for her first job at urbanbelly!

Then there's Tracey Vowell at Three Sisters Garden. We met 17 years ago, when she wasn't even a farmer. She was the chef at Topolobampo. We still talk about that to this day. When Tracey first started coming to Green City as a farmer, she was making deliveries by minivan. She and her partner Kathe had to drive separately, caravan-style, which was really hard for them. So Jackie Shen and I talked about how we could raise money to buy them a proper van. We organized an event with our fellow chefs—I guess you could call it a pop-up—at Red Light where Jackie was the chef. We ended up raising over $10,000 for Tracey and Kathe. Doing things like this for family—that's what Green City Market represents for me.

Of course, I can't talk about the market without talking about Abby Mandel. When I moved back to Chicago after living and working in New York City, and I was back at Trotter's as chef de cuisine, Abby kindly approached me about doing a benefit at Trotter's. Here I was, a month into my job and so nervous because I'd just met Abby and now I asked if we could do the event at our test kitchen next door. And all Charlie said was: "Of course." No hesitation.

I still have Abby's cell phone number in my phone.

We're so fortunate as chefs to have access to these amazing farmers and their food and to be able to support their work. What's been even more valuable and meaningful to me is the community that's developed because of the market. Like I said, they're not farmers to me. They're family.

Award-winning Chef Bill Kim combines a classic culinary education and background in French cuisine with his Korean heritage and experiences growing up in Chicago to create a soulful style of Asian cuisine that is uniquely his own. In 2008, Kim opened urbanbelly, the fast-casual concept specializing in noodles and dumplings, now in Chicago's Wicker Park neighborhood. His first cookbook, *Korean BBQ: How To Master Your Grill in Seven Sauces* was released in April 2018.

Bill Kim
urbanbelly, bellyQ

Abby Mandel left us far too soon. But she did not leave us unprepared or untutored in the way forward for Green City Market or for life.

We first encountered Abby, full force, in the alley between State Street and Wabash—her first tiny start for an outdoor market for local farm fresh food and produce.

She stood nearly alone in those early days, with a friend here or a chef there. But she was at work on a grand mission—to shift our community away from the fast-pace, fast-food, drive-in, nutrition-out, food-in-a-box, farm-in-a-factory world we had become. It was also a world that came with anonymity of connections, most certainly no connection with our food, and no sense of the people who labor to bring it from the earth and to our tables.

Abby was the leader of an early food revolution that would, in time, grow its following locally, and nationwide. She wanted to reset our view of the natural world to what it was meant to be.

So for Abby, **KNOW YOUR FOOD, KNOW YOUR FARMER**, was the anthem she chose when she established the Green City Market in its Lincoln Park home near the zoo where it really began to grow and thrive.

Abby understood the wisdom of John Muir when he said, "when you tug at nature, you find it attached to the rest of the world."

It was the farmers she met, who had a reverence for the land, worked it themselves, and kept the earth clean that were the people she so admired, and from whom she bought the produce herself in those early days when there were too few

customers. She wanted to be sure those farmers went home with money in their pockets and with enough encouragement and hope to believe in their organic agricultural methods to return for another week.

We are certain she had to have taken Carl Sagan's observation to heart: "If you want to make an apple pie from scratch, you must first create the universe."

Abby loved apple pie, and just about anything else, as long as it was made from SCRATCH. She wanted to ensure that every ingredient we used was as close to its natural state as possible. However, you first had to completely remake the way we looked at the food we consumed, but creating a new universe was something Abby had done all her days.

Abby showed that we needed to comprehend the importance of a life lived fully and with meaning, a life that will live on after we are gone. She believed, as with Nature, that the flowers that spring from us, are carried in the seeds we plant.

Abby Mandel was indeed a most prolific planter. Those early seeds grew to a year round GREEN CITY MARKET, a place of joy where we are all connected to the good earth…and to Abby.

Never is that more evident than at the yearly Chefs BBQ. Like any other non-profit organization, the GREEN CITY MARKET needed to raise funds in order to survive. But, this was, after all, a GRASS ROOTS organization and its first notion of just how to stage an event always would start with its supportive friends—the impressive list of Chicago's top chefs and farmers, all willing to donate their talent, time, and food.

Photo by Donna La Pietra

And so was born the Chef BBQ, with scores of chef stations arrayed around the market grounds in Lincoln Park—always on a weekday in July, and starting at 6:00 PM, it turned into one of the hottest tickets in town and created block long lines on Clark Street waiting to get in with the smells of the smoking meats wafting in the summer air.

Any event like this depends on some cooperation from the weather, but it was precisely the lack of cooperation that made one particular Chef BBQ more memorable than all the rest: As all the chefs were doing last minute preps, the bright hot summer sun was beating down, with just minutes before the gates opened. Then, at the stroke of 6 PM, as guests flooded in, a late day torrential thunderstorm with driving rain caused a different sort of flooding—on all the tables that had just been set with dishes and platters of food.

But the story of that downpour was really the resilience of the soaked guests who refused to leave, and the drenched chefs and their staffs at their most inventive selves. You could tell they had years of learning how to remain calm in a kitchen crisis and how to salvage any dish from a near disastrous outcome.

Funny, how we know we will always remember this event and with such affection. We think it's because everyone pulled together to help—where the guests became part of the chef's "line", elbow to elbow, umbrellas up, finding a way to take cover and most of all, cover that food!

We cannot help but feel this is just what Abby had in mind all along: A place of joyous celebration and a coming together around the communal table, where all were connected by a renewed respect for the earth's bounty, and yes, each other.

Donna La Pietra and Bill Kurtis are television journalists and producers. They are passionate conservationists, having created award-winning documentaries on topics spanning a wide range of environmental issues. Both were among the first members of the Board of the Green City Market. They are stewards of 65 acres of land in the north suburbs where they are participating in a field test for growing deep rooted perennial wheat, with the belief that agricultural prairie plants can help save the planet from global warming.

"Green City Market Day" and 10th Anniversary
Rick Bayless, Abby Mandel, Donna La Pietra,
Mayor Richard Daley, Bill Kurtis

Photo courtesy of Donna La Pietra

Abby Schilling
Mick Klug Farm

Looking back at the last twenty years, it is hard to imagine my life without the Green City Market. I was just a teenager when our family started attending, but realized early what an important role it played in our family's livelihood. I had helped my dad both on the farm and at City of Chicago farmers markets since I was a small child, but there was something different about working at the stand at Green City. It was exciting, refreshing…it was something promising. It was also a huge amount of hard work! The convenience provided by having our truck behind our stand was not there, and we learned quickly that getting all of our supplies—tents, tables, weights, produce, etc., from the street to our spot in the park was not easy.

As the years passed, we learned and grew. We became more efficient and were constantly figuring out ways to better serve our customers. Part of that growth included a very important opportunity that Green City Market made available to us: connections to some of the best chefs in the city. Before attending Green City, we had been selling to a few Chicago restaurants, such as Shaw's Crab House and Frontera Grill, but we knew that there was potential to sell to many more amazing establishments. We began to meet chefs as they shopped at our stand at the market. (The Wednesday market was especially hopping with emerging and seasoned chefs alike!) This new outlet for our products was a game-changer, and the relationships we formed with chefs throughout the city were invaluable.

Equally as important as the chef community has been to our farm, are the incredibly supportive market shoppers. The commitment they have to a local and sustainable food system is unwavering. Chatting with, and getting to know, customers twice a week is the best, most special part of my job as a farmer. I like to believe that the relationships between Green City Market vendors and shoppers define the movement: "Know your food. Know your farmer." Without the Green City Market, I do not believe my family's farm would have survived for the future generation to take over. My parents worked tirelessly for many years both on the farm and at farmers markets to make a living and provide for our family. Thankfully, they had an organization that respected their effort and dedication to a difficult farming lifestyle and that supported them beyond measure.

Today, our family continues to be forever grateful to the Green City Market and the opportunities it has provided for vendors, shoppers, and chefs.

We salute Abby Mandel and her vision!

Mick Klug grew up on a 40-acre farm in Berrien County, Michigan that his parents established in the 1930s. He took ownership in 1974, and expanded the land to over 120 acres. For the past several years, Mick has worked closely with his daughter, Abby Schilling, and son-in-law, Mark, successfully sharing management and ownership responsibilities to ensure the land, operations and customer relationships stay within the family. In 2018, Mark's brother, Ben Schilling, and sister-in-law, Bae, joined the team. Mick Klug Farm grows many varieties of fruits and vegetables, employing approximately two dozen employees seasonally. The families are committed to sustainable agriculture and promoting locally grown produce, and Mick Klug Farm is MAEAP verified for its environmentally sound cropping and farmstead systems. The farm has provided fresh produce to the Green City Market for more than fifteen years.

Our founder, Abby Mandel, wanted to create a world-class market for Chicagoans, an idea that seemed so simple, but was absolutely revolutionary at the time. She was tireless in her efforts to bring us the best local, sustainably produced food and succeeded beyond what she could have imagined almost twenty years ago.

Renowned for its farmers and the incredible food they produce, Green City Market has become even more—a family of farmers, chefs, and shoppers. People often tell me that Green City Market is their "happy place," or proudly say that their children have grown up at Green City Market, because this market represents our fundamental roots—how food and communities have always grown together. Our farmers care about the land, the animals, the produce they grow, and the people they feed. Shoppers gather at Green City Market not only to get this marvelous food for their families, but also to connect to others in what is essentially a town square, getting to know each other, sharing recipes, stories, and a smile. Together, they note the passing of time as the produce changes with the seasons—from ramps and asparagus, to mouth-watering summer berries, to the height of tomato season, and finally to the wonderful root vegetables that will keep us warm and cozy through the winter in stews and soups.

Abby knew even more was needed to make a world-class community market, so Club Sprouts and our Edible Gardens were created. At Edible Gardens in Lincoln Park Farm-in-the-Zoo, visitors are welcome to help us plant, weed, and harvest food. Children proudly plant seeds and come all season long to see how their plants are doing and they delight in the excitement of tasting what they have grown come harvest. In our Club Sprouts program, they can taste produce at the peak of its season.

They learn how it is grown and how it gets to them. Those experiments inspired our Edible Education program. We are now teaching students in Chicago schools how to prepare and nourish themselves with local, sustainable crops, inspiring the next generation of eaters to care about how their food is grown and where it comes from.

Our markets and events show that food connects people in ways nothing else can. Wanting all Chicagoans to experience healthy sustainable food, we welcome **Link** at our market. Food is transformative. Everyone should have access.

Celebrating twenty years of Green City Market, we look back fondly at what we have accomplished together. Every farmer, chef, and shopper who has touched the market has made Green City Market the best farmers market in the country. We would not have even opened without our farmers who believe that going back to the basics and growing food with care, love, and concern for the environment is the only way to grow! We would not have succeeded in those early days without the dedication and support of the chefs who took a chance on buying directly from farmers and started a revolution in the food world. We would not be here without every shopper who believes that knowing where their food comes from and how it is grown is vitally important. Together, we are twenty years down and generations to go! I invite you to join us at Green City Market for our next 20 years!

Executive Director of Green City Market since 2015, Melissa Flynn has been honored to carry on the vision of Abby Mandel. Combining years of experience and a passion for community building, her track record of growing a successful business climate is strongly balanced by sustainability.

Melissa Flynn
Green City Market

Holly Mandel Sherr
Abby Mandel

My mom, Abby Mandel, was everything to me—my mentor, parent and best friend. But ever since her death (August 13, 2008) I've realized she was everything to so many.

My mom lost her father at the age of 7. She had two older brothers and her mother. Her mother was lost with the death of her father, so my mom started cooking for the family every night. The meals were simple, but they were homemade by a 7 year old. I can barely fathom. Her love of cooking and entertaining clearly started at a young age.

Abby's passion continued into her young adulthood when she held a benefit for Smith College (her alma mater) in Chicago and Julia Child was the guest of honor. The raffle prize was a Magimix (aka a Cuisinart) and she was the lucky raffle winner! She immediately went home to experiment. She made everything from scratch. Pasta, bagels, yogurt—everything with the Magimix. Her friends reveled in her cooking prowess and begged for tips, instructions, anything. So, as only Abby would, she began teaching cooking classes at the Winnetka Community House.

Soon, she was the talk of the town and everyone wanted the recipes. She very carefully put together a loose leaf binder of her recipes—and as additional classes were scheduled, new recipes could be added. Her moniker would become "Abby cooks and cooks and cooks". And she did! She spent summers in France and Switzerland—honing her skills at the most prestigious Michelin starred restaurants where she would work in the kitchen.

She then went on to work for Cuisinart and became their spokesperson—writing three books with their help. But that was not enough for her. Abby became a member and then president of

Les Dames d'Escoffier Chicago Chapter, wrote weekly columns, "The Weekend Cook", for the Chicago Tribune and also a column for Bon Appétit.

She also became interested in, and a pioneer for, fresh wholesome food with clean local ingredients. Food had become so processed and she had a mission in mind and nothing could get in her way.

In 1989, Abby started the Best of the Midwest Market—a market located at Navy Pier showcasing the best products from the Midwest. It included cheese, Indiana snails, Minnesota venison and a variety of produce. My mom's vision became more focused and stronger as she decided to create an organic fully sustainable market using only local midwestern products. She personally visited all the farms where farmers were interested in joining the market. She wanted to make sure they met the standards she had in mind. Most did not even know the benefits of organic products, as it was such a new and novel topic. The first market opened in an alley in Chicago's Loop in the summer of 1998 with only nine local farmers. In order to entice the farmers to return the following week, my mom would buy any left over products and then she would entertain using all the freshest ingredients that evening.

Abby's energy was boundless and her vision was razor sharp. She is missed every day—but her legacy lives on with the Green City Market!

Residing in New York City, Holly Mandel Sherr is a board member of the Green City Market. Married and the mother of four children, she serves on the NYC Board of JDRF, is a member of the Advisory Board of the Naomi Berrie Diabetes Center and a board member for the Celiac Disease Center at Columbia University.

Photo of Abby Mandel by Carrie Nahabedian

Sharon Hoogstraten
Photography

Edward Smyth Jones
Poetry

Catherine Noback
Illustrations

A SONG OF THANKS

For the sun that shone at the dawn of spring,
For the flowers which bloom and the birds that sing,
For the verdant robe of the gray old earth,
For her coffers filled with their countless worth,
For the flocks which feed on a thousand hills,
For the rippling streams which turn the mills,
For the lowing herds in the lovely vale,
For the songs of gladness on the gale,—
From the Gulf and the Lakes to the Oceans' banks,
Lord God of Hosts, we give Thee thanks!

For the farmer reaping his whitened fields,
For the bounty which the rich soil yields,
For the cooling dews and refreshing rains,
For the sun which ripens the golden grains,
For the beaded wheat and the fattened swine,
For the stallèd ox and the fruitful vine,
For the tubers large and cotton white,
For the kid and the lambkin frisk and blithe,
For the swan which floats near the river banks,
Lord God of Hosts, we give Thee thanks!

For the pumpkin sweet and the yellow yam,
For the corn and beans and the sugared ham,
For the plum and the peach and the apple red,
For the dear old press where the wine is tread,
For the cock which crows at the breaking dawn,
And the proud old "turk" of the farmer's barn,
For the fish which swim in the babbling brooks,
For the game which hide in the shady nooks,—
From the Gulf and the Lakes to the Oceans' banks,
Lord God of Hosts, we give Thee thanks!

For the sturdy oaks and the stately pines,
For the lead and the coal from the deep, dark
    mines,
For the silver ores of a thousand fold,
For the diamond bright and the yellow gold,
For the river boat and the flying train,
For the fleecy sail of the rolling main,
For the velvet sponge and the glossy pearl,
For the flag of peace which we now unfurl,—
From the Gulf and the Lakes to the Oceans'
    banks,—
Lord God of Hosts, we give Thee thanks!

For the lowly cot and the mansion fair,
For the peace and plenty together share,
For the Hand which guides us from above,
For Thy tender mercies, abiding love,
For the blessed home with its children gay,
For returnings of Thanksgiving Day,
For the bearing toils and the sharing cares,
We lift up our hearts in our songs and our
    prayers,—
From the Gulf and the Lakes to the Oceans'
    banks,—
Lord God of Hosts, we give Thee thanks!

May

For the sun that shown at the dawn of spring

For the flowers which bloom and the birds that sing

grass is greener gardens

For the verdant robe of the gray old earth

For her coffers filled with their countless worth

COMPOST!

COMPOST: All paper products and
          Food waste

Recycle: plastic bottles, coffee cup lids

Trash: flatware,
       styrofoam

Not sure? PLEASE

ASK!
Thank you!

47

June

For the flocks which feed on a thousand hills

For the rippling streams which turn the mills

5927 W. Lawrence Ave Tel. (773) 545-7215
Chicago, IL 60630   Fax (773) 427-8632

DANISH
$3 or 2 for 5

MICK KLUG
FARM
ST. JOSEPH · MICHIGAN

Sunflower Sprouts

For the lowing herds in the lovely vale

For the songs of gladness on the gale

July

74

Lamb
Quarters
from
UKINICK

Beet
BABY MICRO GREENS
from
TINY GREENS

SNOW PEA
BABY MICRO GREENS
from
TINY GREENS

Blackberries
from
MICK KLUG FARM

Dill
from
SMITS FARM

YELLOW
Wax Beans
from
LEANING SHED

Arugula
from
GREEN ACRES

For the farmer reaping in his whitened fields

Join Us in the Edible Garden!

9:30 a.m.–12:30 p.m.
Wednesday, Thursday and Saturday

greencity MARKET   Lincoln Park Zoo

The Edible Gardens is a partnership between Green City Market and Lincoln Park Zoo
and is planted and tended by The Organic Gardener Ltd.

For the bounty which
The rich soil yields

From the Gulf and the Lakes to the Oceans' banks

Today's fruit

Blueberries
Cherries
Apricots
Peaches
Plums
Fraise des bois
Raspberries

New:

currants
gooseberries
Sweet & spicy
 - cherry bombs
 - serranos
 - chamomile

A Song of Thanks

August

For the cooling dews and refreshing rains

For the sun which ripens the golden grains

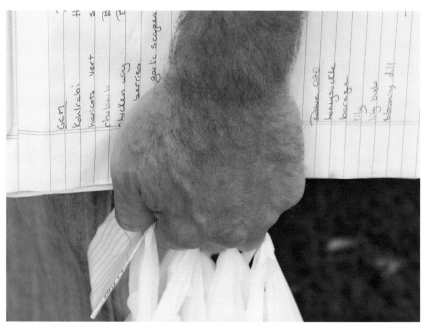

For the bearded wheat and the fattened swine

Eggplant
$2 00
pound

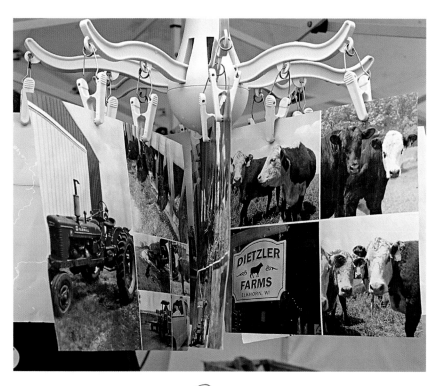

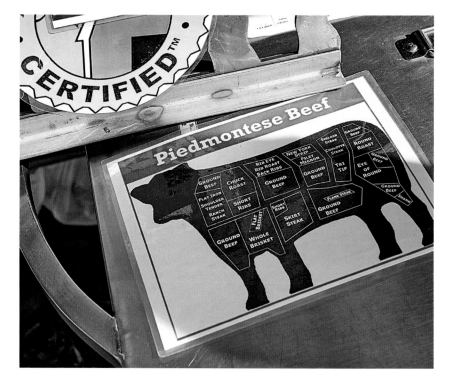

For the stalled ox and the fruitful vine

September

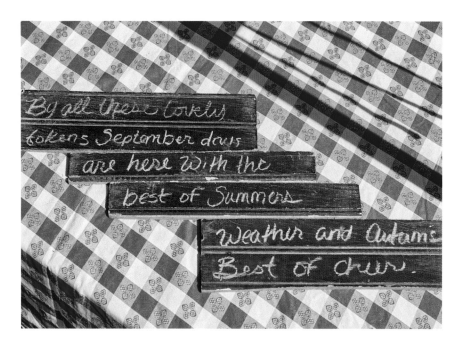

By all these lovely
tokens September days
are here with the
best of Summers
Weather and Autumns
Best of cheer.

BEST
Apples
EVER

For the kid and the lambkin frisk and blithe

Will Trade Flowers for Blackhawk Tickets 815-435-2230

296088 D

For the tubers large and cotton white

Organic
&
Washed:
Baby Arugu
Baby Lettuce
Organic Heirloom
Tomatoe
certified organ

For the swan which floats near the the river banks

138

A Song of Thanks

October

For the pumpkin sweet and the yellow yam

For the corn and beans and the sugared ham

For the plum and the peach and the apple red

For the dear old press where the wine is tread

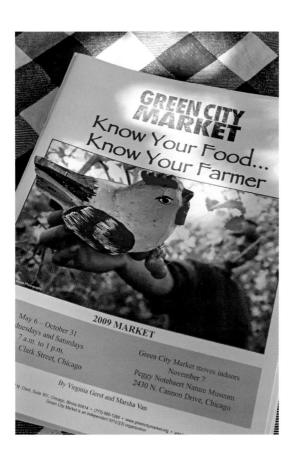

For the cock which crows at the breaking dawn

And the proud old "turk" of the farmer's barn

November

For the fish which swim in the babbling brooks

For the game which hide in the shady nooks

Organic
Rye
$8

-pHlour loaf-
ORGANIC
WHOLE WHEAT
SOURDOUGH
$7

pHlour bakery & cafe

0   7   14
1138 W Bryn Mawr Ave. Chicago, IL 60660 • www.pHlour.com

From the Gulf and the Lakes to the Oceans' banks

A Song of Thanks

For the contributions of the Green City farmers, chefs, and patrons, my Song of Thanks

EDWARD SMYTH JONES

The author,
Edward Smyth Jones

A SONG OF THANKS

For the sun that shone at the dawn of spring,
For the flowers which bloom and the birds that sing,
For the verdant robe of the gray old earth,
For her coffers filled with their countless worth,
For the flocks which feed on a thousand hills,
For the rippling streams which turn the mills,
For the lowing herds in the lovely vale,
For the songs of gladness on the gale,—
From the Gulf and the Lakes to the Oceans' banks,
Lord God of Hosts, we give Thee thanks!

For the farmer reaping his whitened fields,
For the bounty which the rich soil yields,
For the cooling dews and refreshing rains,
For the sun which ripens the golden grains,
For the beaded wheat and the fattened swine,
For the stallèd ox and the fruitful vine,
For the tubers large and cotton white,
For the kid and the lambkin frisk and blithe,
For the swan which floats near the river banks,
Lord God of Hosts, we give Thee thanks!

For the pumpkin sweet and the yellow yam,
For the corn and beans and the sugared ham,
For the plum and the peach and the apple red,
For the dear old press where the wine is tread,
For the cock which crows at the breaking dawn,
And the proud old "turk" of the farmer's barn,
For the fish which swim in the babbling brooks,
For the game which hide in the shady nooks,—
From the Gulf and the Lakes to the Oceans' banks,
Lord God of Hosts, we give Thee thanks!

Concerned that this photographic homage to the Green City Market was in need of structure, I began an exhaustive search for a poem that would suit. Chaucer's sweet "Aprille" may have inspired the tender crops, even so—a bit too hoity-toity. Emily Dickenson had a couple of charming garden verses, but it was Edward Smyth Jones' poem, "A Song of Thanks" that provided the perfect narrative for our market season and the harvest it delivers. The vintage, now public domain, poem added a welcome artistic challenge, and earned my deepest respect. I became curious about the poet's life story. What an amazing saga awaited! I found this excerpted and edited description of his life in the 1993 book, *Blacks at Harvard,* published by New York University Press:

"Edward Smyth Jones was born in Natchez, Mississippi, sometime in March of 1881. His slave parents, Hawk and Rebecca, lacked formal education, but he attended local schools and developed a taste for reading and writing. 1902-03, he studied at nearby Alcorn Agricultural and Mechanical College in exchange for labor. Moving to Indianapolis, Jones won praise for his poetry, but his greatest desire was to attend Harvard. With almost no money in his pocket, he set out in July 1910, hiking, stealing freight-train rides, and sleeping outdoors. He covered 1200 miles and arrived after dark in Harvard Yard, where he found a printer working overtime in the basement of University Hall and asked to see the president. Looking at the dirty and shabby traveler, the printer took him for a crazy tramp and summoned a policeman, who jailed Jones for vagrancy. Arraigned before Judge Arthur P. Stone "93, LL.B. "95, Jones was able to produce letters of congratulation from numerous people including the mayor of Indianapolis, the governor of Indiana and former Vice-President Charles Fairbanks,

along with two of his poems. Jones was released, but not before writing a new poem, "Harvard Square," during his three-day incarceration. Harvard's janitorial supervisor put Jones to work, enabling the would-be student to attend Boston Latin School for a year. During this period, Jones published his second book, *The Sylvan Cabin and Other Verse,* which contained the Harvard poem and bore a dedication to Judge Stone. Lack of funds prevented Jones from entering Harvard, and he moved from place to place until he secured a job as a waiter in the Faculty Club of Columbia University. *The New York Times* published an article about him and lauded his long new poem about the sinking of the Titanic."

The Sylvan Cabin and Other Verse also included the Edward Smyth Jones poem, "A Song of Thanks."

Continuing the search (I have an investigative reporter next door) we found that Jones relocated from New York City to Los Angeles in 1916. By 1920, according to *The Chicago Defender*, Chicago had become his hometown. He reportedly worked as an artist's model and the newspaper finds him still "of Chicago" in 1937. The trail disappears until his death. His last known occupation was "laborer" and Cook County records state that he died on September 28, 1968 at the age of 88.

Most artists, accepting their own inevitable physical departure from this world, fear the disappearance of their works of art. I hope this revival of Edward Smyth Jones' "A Song of Thanks" immortalizes his poetry—just what I would desire for my own work.

Source: *Blacks at Harvard: A Documentary History of African-American Experience At Harvard and Radcliffe* edited by Wernor Sollors, Caldwell Titcomb, Thomas A. Underwood, Randall Kennedy.

Edward Smyth Jones
Poet

"He may not be the best waiter that waits in the Faculty Club, but it would be interesting to know how many better poets eat there."

The New York Times
Published Sunday, February 16, 1913

COLUMBIA FACULTY CLUB SERVED BY COLORED VOTARY OF THE MUSE

Edward Smyth Jones, Who Has Brought Out a Book of Lyrics and Has Had Some Typical Adventures, an Interesting Feature of a Notable Institution.

Sharon Hoogstraten
Shikaakwa Press

Photo by Kim Bartko

*W*hen a country mouse encounters her roots in the big city, as I did when my friend and colleague Kim Bartko suggested that we shoot an essay on Chicago's Green City Market, I was more than interested—I was all in. What photographer can't have fun at a farmers market? Kim knows her way around the local food scene and I got some great shots, so we decided to shoot a whole season, but we still had no idea what a tiger we had by the tail. After eleven years of photography, I submit this retrospective illustrating the beautiful character of the Green City Market. What a trailblazer it has been for all the independent farmers markets and local food movements so familiar today! Citizens and chefs have been inspired by the possibilities of farm-to-table freshness. Unique produce safely grown and delivered is now a standard objective.

I first visited the Green City Market at its new home near Chicago's great lakefront and the Lincoln Park Zoo, and immediately reverted from my adapted big-city self to the sentimental embrace of my Michigan roots. Here were my countrymen; I had to restrain myself from hugging the farmers because I felt like I knew them.

I DO know from beans—my Dutch grandfather used to make me clean bushels of them every year. Along with other Dutchmen from the "Old Country" where he had apprenticed as a meat-cutter, he immigrated to Kalamazoo's familiar low, rich, muck land. Working at Hoekstra's Meat Market, before "snout to tail" became a trendy notion, he was living the concept and sharing the wealth. (Trust me, your social stock can really plummet when you unwrap a headcheese sandwich in the school cafeteria!) His garden provided enough to feed his family of nine children and during the hard times of the 1930's, they raised a cash crop of pansies to bring to market in Chicago.

Like most families of our acquaintance, we "put up" all of our own pickles, tomatoes, vegetables, fruit, jam, and crops from local farms. Foraging from the woods, we stuffed ourselves with all the morels we could eat and filled our Shedd's peanut butter pails with blackberries and wild black raspberries. Every August, Jerry Clinard, pig farmer and family friend, loaded a pickup truck with sweet corn and dumped it in our garage. Assorted kids would spend the day sitting on milk crates and shucking corn, feeling pretty put-upon, never considering our mothers who were sweating over boiling pots and stripping the kernels off with the vicious corn cutter. The laundry baskets bulging with denuded cobs, we drove them back down the hill to slop the hogs. Chest freezers and shelves of Mason jars were commonplace. I don't think I ate a vegetable out of a tin can until I went to college.

Crops defined the pattern of our year. The first rhubarb, gooseberries, morels and asparagus meant another tough winter was behind us. For Memorial Day, we Otsego Cavaliers donned our band uniforms for the march up to the cemetery. Flags and peonies marked the route and every grave. After proper respects were paid, the picnics began—strawberry shortcake, bean salad, sugar-snap peas. When I got fired from my job at the shopping mall, I spent the rest of the summer employed by picking fruit. Blueberries plinking into pails belted unattractively around our waists, or slurping down the juiciest peaches right in the tree. Apple trees were the best for climbing and pears, picked into the galvanized tubs we strapped to our chests, were backbreaking heavy. The farmer's dog bit me in the plum orchard, but the last and hardest crop was Concord grapes— sticky, cold and wet, nasty sharp clippers, and lots of bees. I don't know why, but I loved it. When we carved the pumpkins, the growing season was officially over…another year complete.

These midwestern rural roots are the source of my appreciation for this market and every example of flora and fauna in this book references the Green City Market—even the frog that got an unexpected trip to the bustling metropolis in a flower truck! Shooting before dawn, or across the zoo lagoon, sweet-talking my way on to the rooftop for the view from the Hotel Lincoln helped me define the market in time and place. The harvest provides an indication of the season's progress, as does the attire of the public, but I was also captivated by how distinctly the quality of light changes from spring to mid-summer to autumn. Besides the chapter openers, for each month I've included a double page spread that reflects the atmosphere of that season. The index provides identification to images selected from thousands. Farmers and chefs who autographed the book's end sheets are also present in the body of the book—or at least as many of you as I could fit in!

"A Song of Thanks" written by Edward Smyth Jones in 1911, organized my collection of pretty fruits and vegetables. His poetic praise for the earth's bounty became the script that helped me look beyond the obvious. His verse provided a seasonal timeline and an opportunity to make some small reparation for struggles of circumstance and society that hindered him from reaping a just reward for his poetry.

In Chicago we love to say that if you don't like the weather, wait an hour. There were market days too hot, too cold, or rainy, for dragging my heavy gear around. There were stretches when I just didn't go. Every one of those days these farmers arose before dawn, loaded trucks, and drove to Chicago where they set up their tents and harvest. Observing the market take shape before opening, or breaking down at the end of day, emphasized the huge effort required to bring fresh produce to us city dwellers.

The beautiful produce photographs in this book mirror the pride and artistry of the growers—I was just the appreciative eye. Walking the market with Carrie Nahabedian, she told me this reflected another of Abby Mandel's bright ideas: It's really essential to present the produce in the most visually appealing way possible. Time and again, I marveled at an appetizing arrangement.

I am indebted to the busy chefs and farmers for their exceptional essays, and again to both them, their employees, and the market patrons for their gracious cooperation under my constant camera shadow. I am humbled and honored by all the new friends I have made along this journey—especially Sarah Stegner. Her introductions and enthusiasm got this book off my hard drive.

To my muse, Kim Bartko, I give grateful thanks for initiating this project idea. I'm beholden for the market days when she shared her food community knowledge and for her moral support on shoot days. We have collaborated on many book projects over the years, but this one is a labor of love.

On that note, if love is what kept Robert Gray, husband, proofreader, and in-house supporter, on the job, that would make me one truly lucky girl.

Sharon Hoogstraten is a professional photographer and long-time resident of Chicago. Following her award-winning commercial work for television and print, she is now focused on personal projects, including *Dancing for My Tribe—Potawatomi Tradition in the New Millennium* and *Window on the Square* advocating for the preservation of Chicago's Boulevards. Her Logan Square garden features Aunt Mildred's rhubarb and gooseberries, Grandma Hoogstraten's lilacs, and her dearly departed dad's Michigan dogwood.

Kim Bartko obtains a model release.

Index

Mick Klug Farms rhubarb

Genesis Growers fiddleheads

GCM opening days in May

Morel mushrooms
Hawks Hill Elk Ranch, Joel Espe
Flowering chives

20th Anniversary celebration, 2019
Birthday cake by Bennison's

Earth &Sky Farm, Patty McPhilips

Ellis Farms, René Gelder—the
Dawning of the Age of Asparagus
Tomato Mountain predicts

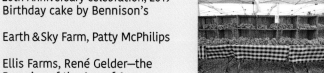

Iron Creek Farm spring greens

Petals tulip mix

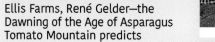

Garden Offerings, Nancy Kapelak

The Winchesters: Emily Berman,
Will Mobley, Colin Morgan

May 20, 2009

Matt's Urban Garden
Paul Friday asparagus

Grass is Greener-Jackie Gennett
with iris, preserved asparagus

Klug strawberries for Eddie Ramos

River Valley Ranch jelly
Mint Creek Farm eggs

The Flower Garden
Garden Gate claytonia
Green Acres radishes
Spring peonies

Nichols amaryllis
GCM Compost Center
Growing Power romaine

Ellis Farm, Memorial Day market

Seedling Farms
Emperor Francis cherries

Mick Klug Farm, Abby and Alicia

Green City Market bags
GCM volunteer badges

Tomato Mountain countdown

June 3, 2009

Granor Farms basil
Iron Creek Swiss chard
Kinnikinnick Farm

Amazing (saltwater) Shrimp Co.
Three Sisters Garden milled corn
Bennison's Bakery bread

Seedling Pineberry strawberry
Delightful Pastries tarts
Klug strawberry delivery

Chamomile

Sweet Pea
The Flower Garden

Growing Home
Leaning Shed garlic scapes
Paul Friday Farm sour cherries

Nordic Creamery
Blue Marble Family Farm
Prairie Fruits Farm & Creamery
Saxon Homestead Creamery
1871 Dairy

Iron Creek Farm tomatoes
Chef Bruce Sherman demo
Hillside Orchards apricots

GCM **Club Sprouts** sign-up
Sunflower sprouts
Green City strawberry contest

Ellis Farms

Everybody got a beat, Baba Eli

Blue Marble, Nick Kirch
Green Acres radishes

July pp.72-83

  pp.84-95

Ellis Farms blueberries

Etta
Chef Stegner and friends
Chef Bayliss and friends
Osterio Via Stato
GCM BBQs - 2015, 2016, 2018

Red, White and Blue

Ellis Farms cherries
Verzenay Patisserie cake
Love-in-a-Mist flowers

Big Star fish, Chef Paul Kahan

Great Lakes Fish
Amazing (saltwater) Shrimp Co.

GCM farmer samples

  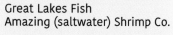

Seedling Farms
Ellis blackberries
Seasons Soda, Bobby Chang
Angie sells Burton's Maple Water

"Bayless Babies" (shirt fronts)

"Education is always in season"
on childrens' tee shirts

Farm-in-the-Zoo Edible Garden

Seedling demo, Peter Klein

Dog loves Genesis green beans

Sunday Dinner burgers with
Heartland Meats

Nichols Farm zuchini blossoms

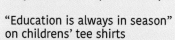 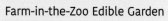 

Joe's Blues, Frank Corrado
Seedling berries & cherries
Floriole Bakery

"Peaches and Honey"

Hillside Galaxy White peach
Chicago Honey Co-op
Flower Garden sunflowers

Green City Market BBQ, 2014

Ellis blueberries—before and after

Green Acres Farm
Costuluto Fiorentino tomato

Nichols sweet corn
Flamin' Fury Peaches
Genesis Growers

GCM "Tomatoes, Melons & More"

Green Acres "Tomato"
Wholesome Harvest "Melons"
Seedling canteloupe
Green Acres Farm has "More"

Bennison Bakery
Prairie Pure Cheese
Heritage Praire Farm organic
wheat berries

Wholesome Harvest

Leaning Shed gladiolas
Nichols Hidden Rose apple
Mists off Lake Michigan

Growing Power

Nichols Farm eggplant varieties

Green Eyed Lady lavender
Green Acres watermelon
Mick Klug Farm blackberries

August 26, 2017

Dietzler Farm
Heartland Meats
Cherry tomato vines

The Flower Garden

Genesis Chinese long beans
Green Acres Farm
Nichols sugar baby melon

Chef Paul Virant shops for Vie
Chef Phillip Foss with list
Blackbird, Chef Paul Kahan

Preserved eggplant recipe with
Chef Chris Pandel, Bristol

Granor Farm vegetables

Abby's Crepes

Joel Masters on bass

August 13, 2008. Green ribbons
for Abby Mandel: Ellis Farm,
Vicki Westerhoff-Genesis Farm,
Nancy Kapelak-Garden Offerings

Three Sisters Garden

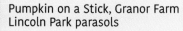

Pumpkin on a Stick, Granor Farm
Lincoln Park parasols

Grass is Greener Autumn poem
Nichols Farm apples
Hoosier Mama Pie Co.
Earth First Farms apple sample

Dogs of the market and...
Chef Paul Kahan

Bennison's Bakery
Sunflower dried seed head

View of GCM across zoo lagoon
Lincoln Park Zoo
Edible Garden, Farm-in-the-Zoo

Seedling watermelon

GCM butter making demo,
Portia Belloc Lowndes

September 5, 2009

Cookies and Carnitas
Becker Lane pork

Nichols Farm canteloupe
The Flower Garden barter

Iron Creek peppers

Leaning Shed cherry tomatoes
American Pride Microfarm
Nichols kale

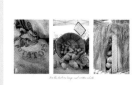

Smits corn, in a potato bag
The next two are potatoes!

Cotton GCM market bag
River Valley fungi t-shirt

Hillside apple
Stony Run Fields sunflower

Annie's Two Foot Band with
Paul Friday and his peaches

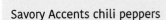

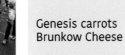

Savory Accents chili peppers

Genesis carrots
Brunkow Cheese

Fresh eucalyptus

Nichols Farm and Orchard
Floriole Bakery
Iron Creek sweet potatoes

Leaning Shed Cider
Seedling Honey Crisp cider
Koval organic spirits

Oriana's Oriental Orchard
Ellis Farms grape varieties

Carrie Nahabedian sniffs celeriac

Growing Power greens
Green Acres pumpkin

Genesis Growers, Vicki Westerhoff

Nichols Farm and Orchard
Capturing the colors of Fall

Iron Creek pumpkins

Sweet Earth Organic Farm corn
Three Sisters Garden black beans
Jake's Country Meats honey ham

Morning set-up

GCM manager Rich Hawley
Tiny Greens and friends
Crumb, Anne Kostroski

Mint Creek Farm
The Flower Garden

Oriana Kruszewski, Asian pears
Hillside Orchards apples

Mick Klug plums
Chef Sarah Grueneberg demo
Flamin' Fury peaches
Seedling apples

October 20, 2012
Rooftop view from Hotel Lincoln

205

November pp. 168–179

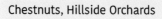

Chestnuts, Hillside Orchards

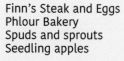

Finn's Steak and Eggs
Phlour Bakery
Spuds and sprouts
Seedling apples

GCM winters at Peggy Notebaert
Radical Root Organic Farm
Inside and out-of-doors

Lake Michigan view at Fullerton
Iron Creek and lakefront detour

Seedling Bartlett pear
Mick Klug apples and pears
Nichols ornamental kale

November 17, 2012

Flower truck stowaway frog
Froggy Meadow Farm, Jerry Boone
Great Lakes Fish
Back of Notebaert Nature Museum

Alden Hills Farms
J's turkeys
J2K Capraio cheeses
Underground Meats
Green Acres brussel sprouts

Outdoor back at Notebaert
Notebaert inside balcony view
Burton's Bourbon maple syrup
Bushel and Peck Preservation

Genesis Growers
Ellis Snow Sweet apples

Thanksgiving snow - 2018

Majestic Nursury birdhouses
Hawks Hill Ranch, Elk antlers

Bob's wild oyster mushrooms

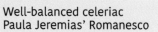

Paul Virant demo feast 2009

Well-balanced celeriac
Paula Jeremias' Romanesco

The End

Seedling
Nichols Farm and Orchard
Chicago, Illinois, USA

GCM 20th Anniversary, 2019

Booklet "The Sylvan Cabin"
by Robert Smyth Jones

New York Times clipping, 1913

Abby Mandel,
photo by Carrie Nahabedian

Tuberose at the market

Leaning Shed "Moulin Rouge"
sunflowers

Ellis Farm fruit baskets

Catherine calls this "bad
sunflower"—I like it.

Please note: The index is
compiled based on memories
and photographic evidence.
Corrections and additions are
most welcome and can be
addressed to:

shikaakwapress@gmail.com

Forget that rhubarb is botanically a vegetable. It's typically used in the same way as acidic fruits. Here, I'm considering it only for desserts, but it's also a great ingredient in savory dishes. Although I was formerly resistant to rhubarb, I'm now an enthusiastic convert.

Abby Mandel

warm rhubarb-strawberry streusel pie

Preparation time: 35 minutes
Cooling time: 1½ hours
Cooking time: 1½ hours

Yield: 8 servings

1½	pounds rhubarb, cut into ⅓-inch-thick slices, about 6 cups
1	pound strawberries, hulled, halved
1½	cups sugar
3	tablespoons quick-cooking tapioca
2	tablespoons orange juice
	Zest of 1 orange
2	teaspoons vanilla extract
¼	teaspoon allspice
¼	teaspoon salt
1	baked, cooled pie crust
1	cup, plus 2 tablespoons flour
⅔	cup packed dark brown sugar
1	stick (½ cup) unsalted butter, chilled, cut into tablespoon-size pieces
1	teaspoon cinnamon

Chicago Tribune column,
Sharon's clipping file

Holly Sherr, Abby Mandel
Photo courtesy of Holly Sherr

! Paul Friday Flamin Fury Peaches!!!

Monika _____ (volunteer)

Orianas Oriental Orchard

CHICAGO HONEY Co-op
SYDNEY BARTON
♡ Jana Kinsman !

THREE SISTERS GARDEN
TRACEY

Eat French
Eat Local !!
VERZÊNAY PÂTISSERIE

BABA E!!
Everybody sotz
A beat sotz

Elis Family Farm
René, Mother, Marc, + Mary and the entire family

Chicago Indoor GARDEN
Tiny Greens (RIA)
Yummi By Nature
Paula Jeremias

Jolis Country Meats

Peter Rauck
River Valley Ranch

GROWING POWER
Will + Erika Allen

IRON CREEK FARM

Smits Farms
André Manti
Melissa Steffang

Tomato Mountain

GROWING HOME

SEEDLING

Green City Market
Junior Board!
Lauren

bushel & peck's

MICK KLUG FARM